SACRAMENTO
C0-BLL-826
Sacramento, CA 95814
12/20

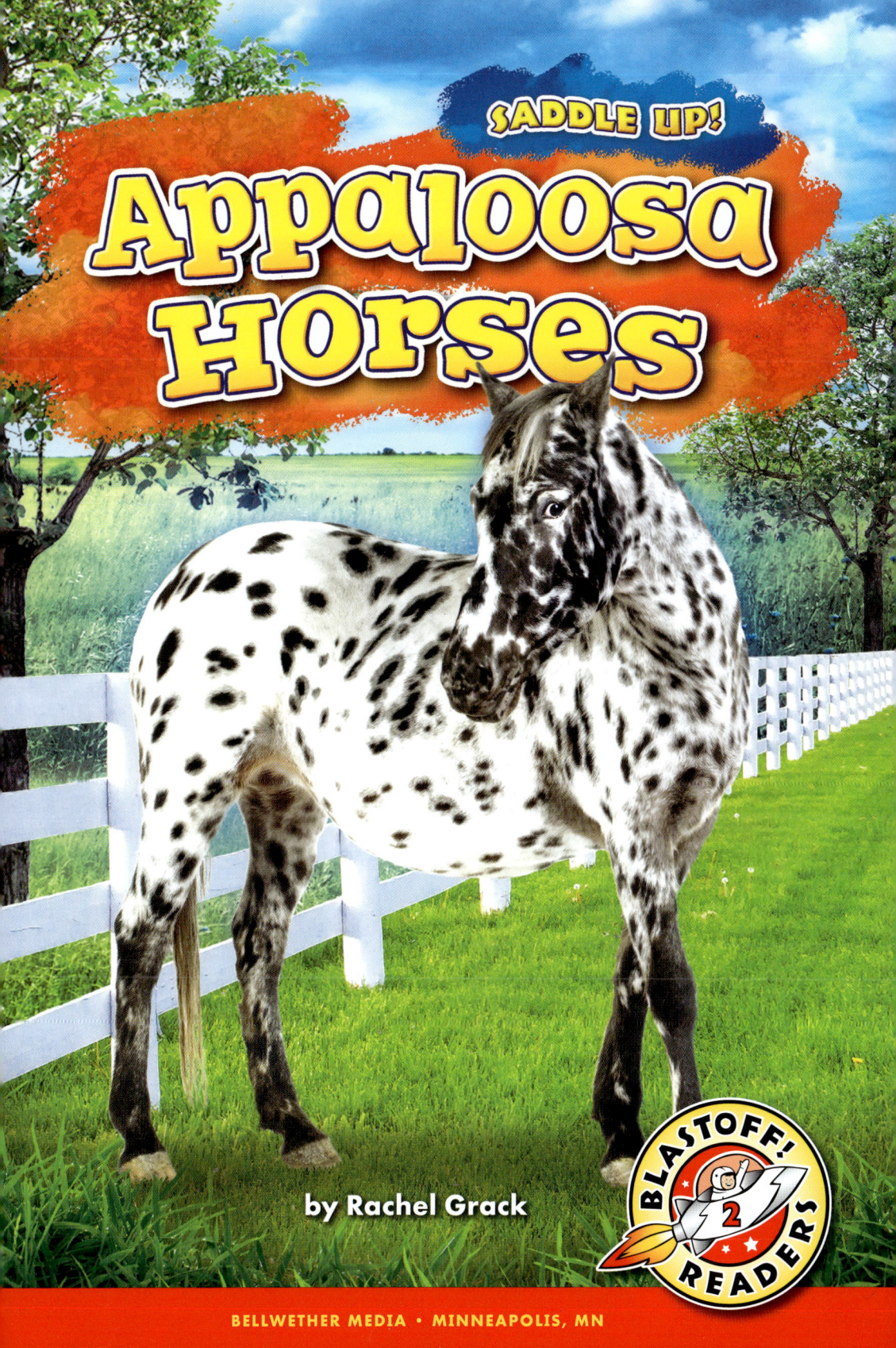

Blastoff! Readers are carefully developed by literacy experts to build reading stamina and move students toward fluency by combining standards-based content with developmentally appropriate text.

 **Level 1** provides the most support through repetition of high-frequency words, light text, predictable sentence patterns, and strong visual support.

 **Level 2** offers early readers a bit more challenge through varied sentences, increased text load, and text-supportive special features.

 **Level 3** advances early-fluent readers toward fluency through increased text load, less reliance on photos, advancing concepts, longer sentences, and more complex special features.

★ **Blastoff! Universe**

Reading Level

 Grade K

 Grades 1–3

 Grade 4

This edition first published in 2021 by Bellwether Media, Inc.

No part of this publication may be reproduced in whole or in part without written permission of the publisher. For information regarding permission, write to Bellwether Media, Inc., Attention: Permissions Department, 6012 Blue Circle Drive, Minnetonka, MN 55343.

Library of Congress Cataloging-in-Publication Data

Names: Koestler-Grack, Rachel A., 1973- author.
Title: Appaloosa horses / by Rachel Grack.
Description: Minneapolis, MN : Bellwether Media, Inc., 2021. | Series: Blastoff! readers: saddle up! | Includes bibliographical references and index. | Audience: Ages 5-8 | Audience: Grades K-1 | Summary: "Relevant images match informative text in this introduction to Appaloosa horses. Intended for students in kindergarten through third grade"–Provided by publisher.
Identifiers: LCCN 2019054253 (print) | LCCN 2019054254 (ebook) | ISBN 9781644872338 (library binding) | ISBN 9781618919915 (ebook)
Subjects: LCSH: Appaloosa horse–Juvenile literature.
Classification: LCC SF293.A7 K64 2021 (print) | LCC SF293.A7 (ebook) | DDC 636.1/3-dc23
LC record available at https://lccn.loc.gov/2019054253
LC ebook record available at https://lccn.loc.gov/2019054254

Text copyright © 2021 by Bellwether Media, Inc. BLASTOFF! READERS and associated logos are trademarks and/or registered trademarks of Bellwether Media, Inc.

Editor: Elizabeth Neuenfeldt   Designer: Andrea Schneider

Printed in the United States of America, North Mankato, MN.

Table of Contents

Easy to Spot!	4
Spots and Stripes	6
Appaloosa Beginnings	12
Outstanding Horses	18
Glossary	22
To Learn More	23
Index	24

Easy to Spot!

Appaloosa horses are beautiful animals from the United States.

They are known for their spotted **coats**. These horses stand out wherever they go!

Spots and Stripes

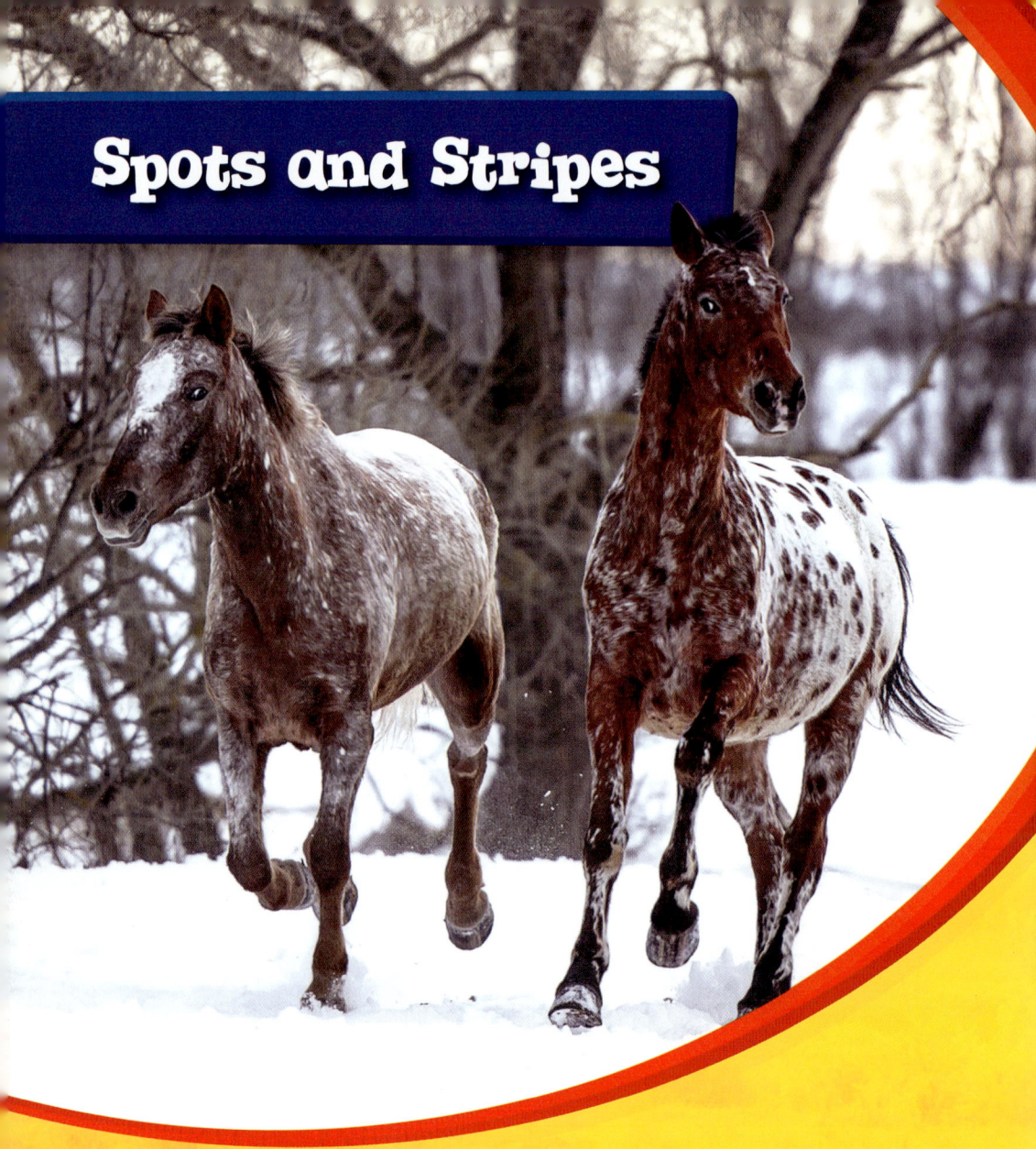

Appaloosas can be a mix of many different colors and spotted **patterns**.

Some horses have a few spots. Others have spots everywhere!

Coat Patterns

blanket

spots

blanket with spots

Appaloosas have **mottled** skin on their faces. The white part of their eyes shows all the time.

mottled skin

Their **manes** are short and thin.

Appaloosas are between 14 and 16 **hands** high.

They stand on strong, hard **hooves**. These colorful horses also have striped hooves!

striped hoof

Size of an Appaloosa Horse

20 hands

14 to 16 hands

12 hands

10 hands

0 hands

one hand = 4 inches (10 centimeters)

Appaloosa Beginnings

Palouse River

In the 1700s, the **Nez Percé** started the Appaloosa **breed**.

The Nez Percé lived near the Palouse River. Appaloosas are named after this river!

Nez Percé homeland

The Nez Percé used Appaloosas for hunting and traveling.

They wanted the fastest and strongest horses. They **bred** only the best Appaloosas.

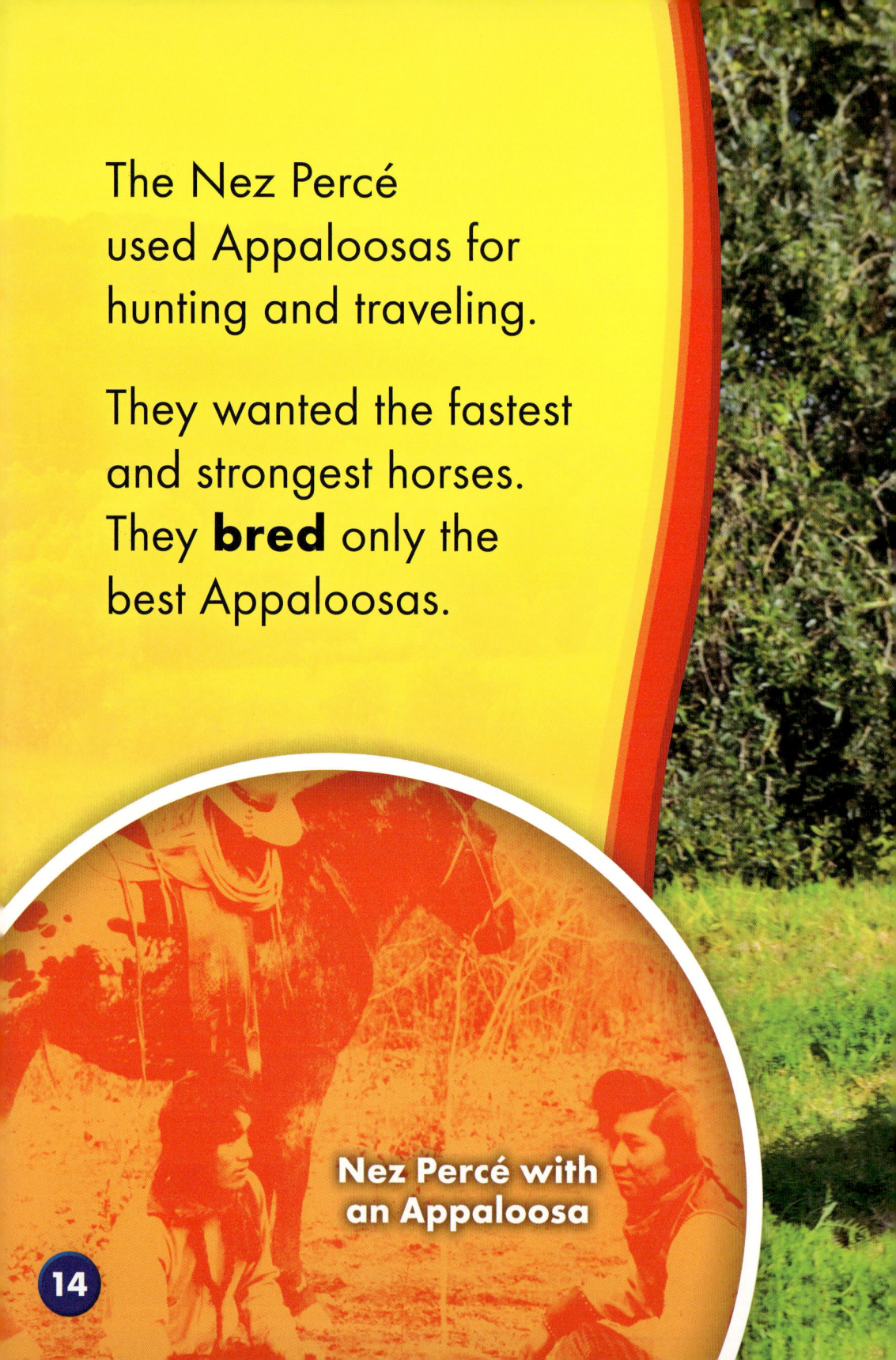

Nez Percé with an Appaloosa

In 1877, the Nez Percé lost their homeland in a war. Many horses died.

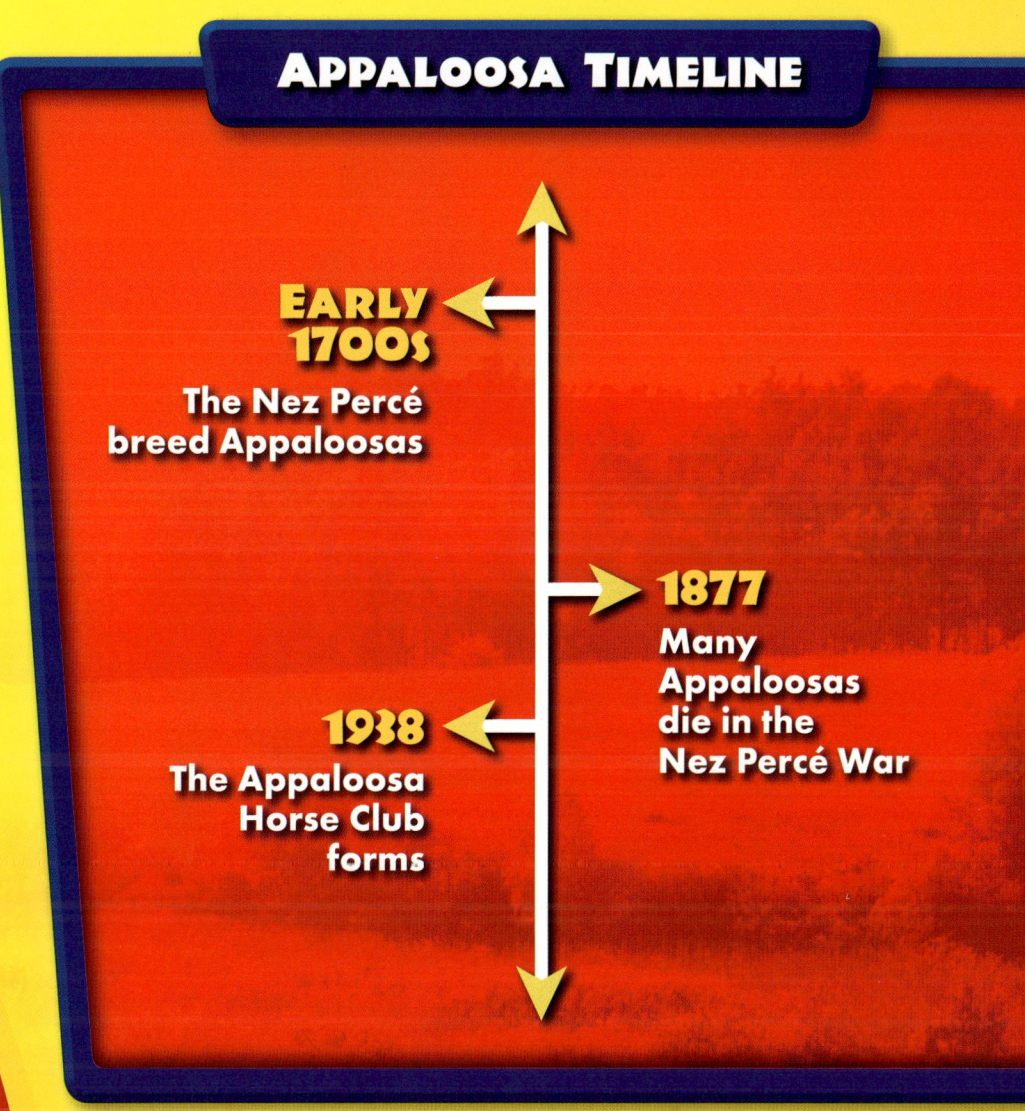

In 1938, the Appaloosa Horse Club formed. The club saved the breed!

Outstanding Horses

jumping

Appaloosas are **agile** and easy to train. They make top show horses for **dressage** and jumping.

Their beauty and skill stand out everywhere they **trot**!

Horsing Around
TROTS

- passage trot
- medium trot
- extended trot

Today, more than 635,000 Appaloosas live around the world.

They are quick, strong, and tireless. These horses also make great friends!

Glossary

agile—fast and graceful

bred—purposely mated two horses to make horses with certain qualities

breed—a certain type of horse

coats—the hair or fur covering some animals

dressage—a horse show event judged on movement, balance, and the ability to follow directions

hands—the units used to measure the height of a horse; one hand is equal to 4 inches (10 centimeters).

hooves—the hard coverings on the feet of animals such as horses and pigs

manes—hair that grows from the necks of horses

mottled—spotted

Nez Percé—a Native American group from what is now Idaho, Washington, and Oregon

patterns—the markings of an animal's fur

trot—to move faster than walking but slower than running; when horses trot, a front leg moves at the same time as an opposite back leg.

To Learn More

AT THE LIBRARY
Grack, Rachel. *American Paint Horses*. Minneapolis, Minn.: Bellwether Media, 2021.

Meister, Cari. *Appaloosa Horses*. Mankato, Minn.: Amicus Ink, 2019.

Noll, Elizabeth. *Appaloosa Horses*. Mankato, Minn.: Black Rabbit Books, 2019.

ON THE WEB
FACTSURFER

Factsurfer.com gives you a safe, fun way to find more information.

1. Go to www.factsurfer.com.
2. Enter "Appaloosa horses" into the search box and click 🔍.
3. Select your book cover to see a list of related content.

Index

Appaloosa Horse Club, 17
bred, 14
breed, 12, 17
coats, 4, 7
colors, 6, 10
dressage, 18
eyes, 8
faces, 8
homeland, 13, 16
hooves, 10
hunting, 14
jumping, 18
manes, 9
mottled skin, 8
name, 13

Nez Percé, 12, 13, 14, 16
Palouse River, 12, 13
patterns, 6, 7
size, 10, 11
spots, 4, 6, 7
timeline, 17
train, 18
traveling, 14
trot, 19
United States, 4
war, 16

The images in this book are reproduced through the courtesy of: Eric Isselee, front cover (horse); Vova Shevchuk, pp. 2, 3, 23 (horseshoes); Greg Balfour Evans/ Alamy, p. 4 (inset); rokopix, pp. 4-5; olgaru79, pp. 6-7; bob langrish/ Alamy, p. 7 (blanket); Nicole Ciscato, p. 7 (spots); Mark J. Berrett/ Alamy, p. 7 (blanket with spots); Olga_i, p. 8; dotana, pp. 8-9; Bettina Calder, p. 10 (inset); Zuzana Burá ová/ Alamy,pp. 10-11; Don Grall/ Getty Images, pp. 12-13; Wikipedia, p. 14 (inset); BronwynMack, pp. 14-15; Science History Images/ Alamy pp. 16-17; Margo Harrison, pp. 18-19; blickwinkel/ Alamy, p. 20; cynoclub, pp. 20-21.